2

Congratulations! You are holding in your hands one of the most effective tools for test preparation available. The effectiveness of flashcards joined with the convenience and ease of use of a book. We want to offer a quick reminder about how these flashcards are set up and what you can expect.

As you will see, there are two "sets" of flashcards. The top set has a grey background. The bottom set has plain white background. In either case, the question is on the right page and you simply flip the page to see the answer, just like with a traditional flashcard. We highly suggest working through one set at time.

As you will notice, there are different types of questions on the flashcards. None are intended to necessarily be "harder" or "easier", but instead intended to challenge you in different ways. Some have multiple choice questions, which will allow you to think critically as well as get practice for the style of questions you will encounter on the exam. Other flash cards however will provide no clues! This will require you to mentally recall information on your own without the benefit of seeing possible answer choices.

The goal is to engage your brain in different ways so that your studying time is as effective as possible and you retain the necessary information for the test. Unlike with rote memorization or simply reading from a book, you will not experience brain-drain and lose information because you mind is actively engaged the entire time. Less studying, but greater retention of information!

With that, let's get started on the next page. Simply read the question and flip the page to see if you got it right. Remember, work across the entire top (grey) set first, then come back to page 1 and start the bottom (white) set.

Good luck, and again congratulations on your upcoming fantastic test score!

Which mechanism is most closely associated with best practices?
- A. Measurable criteria
- B. Disease specificity
- C. Benchmarking
- D. Syndrome specificity

What are the roles of a case manager?

C.
Best practices are defined as those processes that have proven to be, in comparison to other practices, the best in terms of many aspects including appropriateness, effectiveness, and timeliness. They are identified as such because of their leading benchmarks. Case managers should be aware of these benchmarked best practices to identify better ways of doing things and to compare their performance to leaders in the field.

Clinician, change agent, consultant, coordinator and facilitator of care, supervisor of care, educator of staff and clients, leader, manager, negotiator, advocate, researcher, quality improvement coordinator, risk manager, financial and reimbursement expert, and utilization and resource manager.

Which American Nurses Association *Standard of Practice* is fulfilled when critically evaluating and developing evidence-based practices?
- A. Resource utilization
- B. Facilitation
- C. Collaboration
- D. Research

What are the role dimensions and functions of a nursing case manager?

D.
Evidence-based practices are based on valid and sound research, which is one of the American Nurses Association's Standards of Practice and also a role of the nursing case manager. These evidence-based practices allow case managers to evaluate and use them to improve the quality of client care when they are applicable to client conditions and preferences.

Financial and business, information management and communication, professional development, clinical and patient care, and management and leadership

Which phase of the nursing process is most similar to the assessment phase?
- A. Nursing diagnosis
- B. Planning
- C. Implementation
- D. Evaluation

What are the underlying principles and core values of case management?

D.

The evaluation phase of the nursing process is most similar to the assessment phase of the nursing process. Both of these phases consist of data collection relating to the client's biological, psychological, social, spiritual, and cultural status. The primary difference between these two phases is the purpose of this data collection. Assessment data is collected to generate a nursing diagnosis and a plan of care; evaluation data is collected to evaluate the outcomes of care when contrasted with the pre-established expected outcomes determined during the planning phase.

- Believing that case management, through advocacy, improves client health, wellness, and autonomy
- Recognizing and upholding people's rights to dignity, respect, worth, and other basic rights
- Committing to quality outcomes for all clients in a supportive, empowering environment with the appropriate use of resources
- Recognizing that justice, non-maleficence, autonomy, and beneficence guide the ethical principles of case management
- Firmly believing that the client, family, reimbursement systems, and healthcare team can achieve optimal functioning and wellness for the client

Karen Zander advanced which model of case management?
A. Collaborative Practice Model
B. ProACT Model
C. Triad Model
D. Beth Israel Multidisciplinary Patient Care Model

What are the ANA's Standards of Care?

A.

Karen Zander advanced the Collaborative Practice Model of case management. This model is interdisciplinary and collaborative among members of a healthcare team. Critical pathways and case management plans are used; variance, variance analysis, and evaluation are also incorporated into this model.

Assessment, nursing diagnosis, outcomes identification, planning, implementation, and evaluation

Which case management model differentiates the roles of the registered nurse into a primary nurse role and a case manager role?
  A. Collaborative Practice Model
  B. Triad Model
  C. Beth Israel Multidisciplinary Patient Care Model
  D. ProACT Model

What are the ANA's Standards of Practice?

D.

The Robert Wood Johnson University Hospital's ProACT Model differentiates the roles of the registered nurse into a primary nurse role and a case manager role. For the registered nurse to take on this additional role, the nursing department is restructured to maximize supportive and ancillary services.

Quality of care, performance appraisal, education, ethics, collaboration, research, and resource allocation

An example of a client-oriented outcome that is appropriate in terms of nursing case management is:
A. The case management plan will be effective.
B. The client will be free of any complications.
C. There will be no variances during the length of stay.
D. The client will be informed about his/her disease process.

True or False: The nursing process is a client-centered, dynamic, systematic, goal-oriented problem solving approach to nursing care.

B.
An example of a client-oriented outcome that is appropriate in terms of nursing case management is, "The client will be free of any complications." "The client will be informed of his/her disease process" is not an outcome; instead, it reflects a process and an intervention. The other outcomes are not client-oriented.

True

Which characteristic of a well-developed expected outcome is the most useful to data collection and research?

A. Client-oriented
B. Specificity
C. Achievability
D. Measurability

What are the steps of the nursing process?

D.

Appropriately developed expected outcomes, or goals, are client-oriented, specific, achievable, realistic, and measurable. It is measurability that is useful for data collection and research. For example, data collection, quality improvement activities, and formal research can be conducted using a measurable outcome such as the absence of nosocomial infections. The SMARTTA (*specific*, *measurable*, *achievable*, *realistic*, *time frame*, *trackable*, and *agreed* to by the client) framework can be used for setting goals.

Assessment, diagnosis, planning, implementation, and evaluation

What is the primary purpose of the evaluation of client outcomes?

A. To maximize reimbursement rates and to decrease lengths of stay
B. To improve the effectiveness and quality of the care provided
C. To ensure the proper allocation of limited resources and services
D. To avoid reimbursement denials and fraud accusations

What are some of traits that characterize critical thinkers?

B.

The primary purpose of the evaluation of client outcomes is to improve the effectiveness and quality of the care provided. Evaluation data, on an individual or aggregated basis, is necessary to facilitate this essential case management function and responsibility.

Confidence, courage, tolerance for ambiguity, perseverance, curiosity, autonomy, intellectual expertise, high levels of motivation, and open-mindedness

Variance analysis is closely associated with which case management role dimension?
A. Professional development dimension
B. Financial and business dimension
C. Information management dimension
D. Both B and C

What are the steps of decision-making?

D.

Variance analysis is most closely associated with both the financial and business dimension and the information management dimension of the case management role. For example, variance analysis is used to aid decision making relating to cost control and utilization/resource management. The professional development dimension relates to personal and staff development activities to facilitate successful case management and competency.

- Identifying and defining the problem and purpose of the decision making
- Establishing criteria relating to the desired decision
- Ranking and weighing the criteria in terms of their importance
- Exploring the possible alternatives according to the established criteria
- Determining the best alternative based on the consideration of potential benefits versus potential risks
- Making the decision or course of action
- Evaluating the outcome of the decision in terms of its effectiveness

Which of these is a characteristic of a critical thinker?
- A. Problem solving
- B. Decision making
- C. Curiosity
- D. Both A and B

What are the steps of problem-solving?

C.
Some of the traits that characterize good critical thinkers are curiosity, courage, tolerance for ambiguity, perseverance, autonomy, intellectual expertise, high levels of motivation, and open-mindedness. Problem solving and decision making require critical thinking and professional judgment, but they are not characteristics of a critical thinker; instead, they are outcomes of critical thinking.

- Defining the problem
- Collecting data
- Analyzing data
- Generating possible solutions to the problem
- Selecting the best possible solution
- Implementing the solution or planned change
- Evaluating the result of the implemented solution

The most commonly occurring problem-solving failures result from a lack of accurate _____.

A. Data analysis
B. Problem definition
C. Benefit-risk analysis
D. Evaluation of outcomes

When do conflicts arise?

B.
The most commonly occurring cause of problem-solving failures is a failure to clearly define the problem. A clear and complete definition of the problem, which does not reflect any symptoms of the problem, allows problem solvers to effectively begin the problem-solving process.

When there are disparate opinions, values, beliefs, and/or attitudes

Which of the following nursing diagnoses most significantly impacts the case manager's role?
A. Fatigue related to the effects of chemotherapy
B. Disturbed body image related to hair loss
C. Diarrhea related to the effects of irradiation therapy
D. Risk for impaired skin integrity related to the effects of irradiation therapy

What are the types of conflict?

D.
The risk of impaired skin integrity related to the effects of irradiation therapy is the nursing diagnosis that most significantly impacts the case manager's role. Complications include skin breakdown, impact on costs, and lengths of stay. Although all of the other nursing diagnoses are considered by the case manager, complications are a priority consideration.

Intrapersonal (ethical or moral), interpersonal, and organizational (interdepartmental)

Nurses who are facilitating self-care in terms of insulin administration are employing teaching related to which domain?

A. Psychological
B. Psychomotor
C. Cognitive
D. Affective

What is the best way to resolve conflicts?

B.
The psychomotor domain addresses hands-on skills such as insulin administration, use of crutches, and correct use of a blood glucose monitor. The cognitive domain is the knowledge domain, and the affective domain addresses values, attitudes, and beliefs.

To have the group discuss their beliefs and attitudes and then negotiate a resolution under the guidance of the case manager

Select the teaching strategy that is correctly paired with its domain of learning.
A. Discussion—Cognitive
B. Discussion—Psychomotor
C. Demonstration—Cognitive
D. Demonstration—Affective

True or False: Coercion is a useful way to solve conflict.

A.

Discussion, one-to-one and in groups, is an appropriate teaching strategy, or methodology, for the cognitive domain of the teaching/learning process. Demonstration and return demonstration are appropriate teaching strategies, or methodologies, for the psychomotor domain of the teaching/learning process.

False. Coercion is NOT a useful way to solve conflict; collective communication and collaboration is.

Select the correct term for adult learning that is correctly paired with a strategy that should be used for this kind of learning.

A. Pedagogy—Active learner involvement
B. Pedagogy—Learner involvement in the planning phase
C. Andragogy—Passive learner involvement
D. Andragogy—The potential for immediate application of the learning

_____ and _____ are essential to care driven by medical need, are appropriate, are efficient, and are consistent with the guidelines and criteria established with third-party payers including Medicare and Medicaid.

D.
Pedagogy is childhood learning; andragogy is adult learning. Unlike pedagogy, adult learning has immediate usefulness in terms of solving problems; it requires active learner involvement and participation, and the curriculum and content are based on learner needs and desires. Pedagogy lacks these elements.

Healthcare utilization and resource allocation

Which theorists developed the Seven Phases of Change Theory?
   A. Lewin, Watson, and Westley
   B. Lippitt, Watson, and Westley
   C. Lewin, Havelock, and Orem
   D. Havelock, Westley, and Rogers

_____ is a retrospective review of whether or not the care was provided in the most effective and efficient manner.

B.
Lippitt, Watson, and Westley developed the Seven Phases of Change Theory. These seven phases are: client awareness of the need for change, development of a change agent/client relationship, problem defined, goals established, plan for change implemented, change accepted, and change agent/client relationship changed.

Utilization review

Havelock developed which change theory?
A. Seven Phases of Change Theory
B. Force Field Analysis Theory
C. Six Phases of Change Theory
D. Innovation-Decision Process Theory

_____ is a prospective, proactive manner that ensures (before the care is rendered) that effective and efficient care will be given.

C.
Havelock developed the Six Phases of Planned Change Theory. These phases are developing relationships, diagnosing the existing problem, collecting available resources, choosing a solution, garnering acceptance, and stabilizing the change. Lewin developed Force Field Analysis; Rogers developed the Innovation-Decision Process; and Lippitt, Watson, and Westley developed the Seven Phases of Change Theory.

Utilization management

When clients are able to understand health-related information and are able to use it to make appropriate healthcare decisions, they are considered _____.
A. Health literate
B. Competent
C. Knowledge-based
D. Motivated

Utilization management consists of which four strategies?

A.

Patients are considered "health literate" when they are able to understand information and use it to make appropriate healthcare decisions. Almost 50% of patients are NOT health literate.

Demand management, utilization review, case management, and disease management

An appropriate learning objective for a client can be:

A. The case manager will teach the client how to cough and breathe deeply after surgery.
B. The case manager will help the client understand diabetes and the diabetic diet.
C. The client will list the components of a healthful diabetic diet.
D. The client will appreciate the importance of regular exercise and a healthful diet.

What are the utilization review criteria?

C.

Learning objectives must be measurable, specific, behavioral, learner-centered, consistent with assessed need, and congruent with the domain of learning. An appropriate learning objective for a client can be "The client will list the components of a healthful diabetic diet." Choices A and B are case manager-oriented and not client-centered. The learning objective "The client will appreciate" is not measurable.

The need for medical physician services (daily visits, operative procedures, and/or assessments and orders for treatment), which justify acute care; the need for skilled nursing care (professional decision making, observation, and complex treatments and procedures), which also justifies acute care; and the provision of other treatments and services (that are appropriate surgical procedures only with major anesthesia; dangerous diagnostic tests such as cardiac catheterizations; and unstable, unpredictable biopsychosocial needs and conditions).

The case manager has initiated client-teaching classes relating to chronic obstructive pulmonary disease (COPD). The case manager looks at the lengths of stay data among those patients who have participated in this class and notes that the lengths of stay among them are less than those for clients who did not attend the class. Which type of evaluation has this case manager used?

A. Formative
B. Summative
C. Process
D. Planning

_____ provide objective ways to verify insurance benefits and coverage (before admission); to determine if the admission is medically necessary and appropriate as the only sound alternative; to ensure the requirements and procedures for the managed care program are met; to enable the identification, prevention, and resolution of quality care issues that can adversely affect the client, the anticipated discharge plan and length of stay, and the indicated level of care.

B.
Summative evaluation occurs after the learning activity. It can include patient outcome data and determining whether or not the education has achieved the established learning objectives for the individual or group. Formative evaluation is completed while the educational activity is being implemented.

Utilization review criteria

Which statement about certification is accurate as related to nursing case managers?

A. Certification is mandatory and recommended for case managers.
B. Certification is mandatory for nursing case managers, but not for other case managers.
C. Licensure is mandatory, but certification is not mandatory for nursing case managers.
D. Licensure and certifications are very similar; they both validate specialized competency.

What is the primary purpose of utilization?

C.
Licensure is mandatory for nurses to work as nursing case managers, but certification is not mandatory. It is voluntary, but highly recommended. Licensure is very different from certification in many ways including the fact that licensure validates basic nursing competency whereas certification validates advanced and specialized nursing competency.

To ensure reimbursement

Where can a nurse find the scope of practice for a licensed practical (or vocational) nurse and a registered nurse?

A. In the law
B. In an American Nurses Association publication
C. On the back of an LPN or RN license
D. In a healthcare facility's policy manual

_____, as based on medical necessity, indicates that the admission of a client to a specific level of care (acute hospital, other inpatient facility, sub-acute setting, rehabilitation setting) has been deemed appropriate based on the current, documented needs of the client.

A.
You can find the scope of practice for a licensed practical (or vocational) nurse and a registered nurse in the law. Scopes of practice are legislative initiatives that all states in the U.S. have. Although there could be some differences among states, for the most part, states' scopes of practice are very similar.

Pre-admission insurance authorization

Which of the following is the primary purpose of documentation?
A. Reimbursement
B. Avoidance of lawsuits
C. Evaluation of care
D. Communication

_____, or ongoing authorizations, are requested throughout the client's course of care and treatment. These concurrent authorizations are necessary to ensure adequate reimbursement for comorbidities and unanticipated client needs that have occurred since the client was admitted with the pre-certification.

D.
The primary purpose of documentation is communication. Good documentation facilitates optimal and timely communication among team members; complete and appropriate care; prevention of errors of omission, commission, and duplication; timeliness of care; and minimization of treatment delays.

Concurrent authorizations

Documentation is used for reimbursement because:
A. The JCAHO requires it.
B. Individual state departments of health require it.
C. ICD 9 codes are based on it.
D. ICD 2013 codes are based on it.

_____ does not ensure reimbursement; it simply indicates that the authorization is being considered. The final decision can approve, partially approve, or completely refuse to authorize care or services.

C.

ICD 9 medical codes for reimbursement are based on documentation. If it is not documented, it was not completed; and if it was not completed, there is no reimbursement. Documentation is essential to the financial viability of healthcare facilities. Documentation is mandated by Medicare's Conditions of Participation, the JCAHO, and individual state departments of health.

Pending authorization

Which law protects the client's rights in terms of privacy and confidentiality of medical records and information?
   A. Privacy of Information Act
   B. Patients' Bill of Rights Act
   C. Health Insurance Privacy and Accountability Act
   D. Health Insurance Portability and Accountability Act

True or False: As soon as acute care criteria are no longer met, the client should be discharged, or a denial will be highly possible.

D.

The Health Insurance Portability and Accountability Act (HIPAA) is the federal law that protects patients' rights to privacy and confidentiality for all medical information, including electronic information, unless the client has consented to it in writing. The Patient Bill of Rights is not legislation.

True

Which of the following is NOT one of the four components of malpractice?
A. Intentionality
B. Owed duty
C. Breached duty
D. Consequential injury

What are some preventive strategies for the nursing case manager?

A.
Malpractice consists of four elements: damages to the patient, duty owed to the patient, duty that was breached, and direct or indirect breach-caused injuries and damages. Malpractice can be intentional or unintentional.

Negotiating and communicating with the payer by clearly, objectively, and accurately presenting the case and specifically asking the payer which criteria are the bases of his/her denial or possible denial.

Your client has a guardianship with a family member. What is the reason underlying this guardianship?

A. The client is elderly or at the end of his/her life.
B. The client is not competent enough to make decisions.
C. The client is too sick to make decisions.
D. The family member financially supports the client.

What is the primary reason to document all aspects of communication with an insurance provider?

B.

Guardianship, also referred to as conservatorship, refers to the legal process with which another person makes decisions for a person who is not competent enough to make sound decisions on his/her own.

To provide the basis for a future appeal of the denial

Which statement about advanced directives is accurate?

A. Advanced directives are a legally binding document.

B. Advanced directives list only the things the client does not want.

C. Advanced directives are essentially the same as conservatorships.

D. Advanced directives should be done after a person is diagnosed with a terminal disease.

True or False: Denials do not significantly affect the facility's financial status and viability.

A.

Advanced directives are legally binding documents. This document contains the wishes of the client in terms of the treatments and interventions that he/she does _and_ does not want carried out when he/she is no longer able to competently provide these consents and rejections.

False. Denials DO significantly affect the facility's financial status and viability.

Compliance officers are most concerned with
_____.

A. Malpractice
B. Negligence
C. Medical records
D. Fraud

What is the primary purpose of appeals?

D.

Compliance officers strive to prevent fraud. Fraud is a serious offense that has serious consequences.

To recover the costs of rendered care and services

Which of the following specifically protects "whistle blowers" who report fraud?
   A. False Claims Act
   B. Qui Tam provisions
   C. Mandatory Reporting Act
   D. Case Manager Standards of Practice

What are some of the components of a successful appeals process?

B.

The "whistle blower," or Qui Tam, provisions of the False Claims Act specifically protects "whistle blowers" who report fraud and violations of the False Claims Act. Some violations of this law include kickbacks and billing for services that were not provided.

Clear and current payer criteria, establishing and maintaining appropriate contact personnel, response mechanisms, quality measures, and team member education and training

The Code of Professional Conduct for Case Managers contains eight principles, one of which addresses the case manager's role in terms of:
- A. Mandatory reporting of child abuse
- B. Mandatory reporting of elder abuse
- C. Collaboration
- D. Billing and coding

What are some of the commonly occurring denials, or non-certifications, that case managers address?

C.

The eight principles of the Code of Professional Conduct for Case Managers requires that the case manager collaborate with others, among other things such as maintaining one's competency and upholding the client's right to dignity. The reporting of elder and child abuse and medical billing and coding are not included.

Partial payments and no payments for services, support services, durable medical equipment, medications, and increased lengths of stay

Which ethical principle is the case manager demonstrating when he/she provides client care in a safe and high-quality manner?

A. Competency
B. Fidelity
C. Veracity
D. Justice

What is the time interval in which an appeal must be filed?

C.

The case manager is demonstrating veracity when he/she provides client care in a safe and high-quality manner. Veracity is being faithful and true to one's professional promises and responsibilities by providing high-quality, safe care in a competent, scientifically grounded manner. Competency is not an ethical principle. Veracity is truthfulness, and the principle of justice requires fairness to all. For example, limited resources must be fairly and justly distributed among all patients.

Within 30-60 days of a denial notification. Insurance companies must then respond to that appeal within 30-60 days after the appeal is filed. The outcomes of appeals can result in full acceptance and reimbursement, partial acceptance and reimbursement, or no acceptance or reimbursement.

When nursing case managers facilitate client decision making without coercion, they are upholding the client's right to _____.

A. Fidelity
B. Veracity
C. Justice
D. Self-determination

Timely _____ ensures not only desired clinical outcomes, but also solid financial outcomes for the organization.

D.
Autonomy and self-determination are the rights of the client to make choices and decisions without coercion and undue influence of others. Case managers do not impose their own beliefs, values, or opinions on the client; they accept all client choices without judgments.

discharge

As legally mandated reporters, nursing case managers must report:
- A. All suspected child abuse
- B. Clinically proven child abuse
- C. Sexual harassment
- D. Variances of care

Discharge planning should begin with admission and include which essential elements of success?

A.
Nursing case managers must report all suspected cases of child abuse. It does not need to be clinically proven. It is the role of law enforcement personnel to investigate and determine if abuse has occurred.

- Establishing an anticipated discharge date
- Identifying family members and significant others who are willing, available, and physically and cognitively able to provide necessary support to the client upon discharge
- Collaborating with the patient, physicians, family members, and other team members to collectively determine the anticipated discharge date and work to achieve that goal
- Conducting multidisciplinary discharge rounds

Healthcare utilization and resource allocation historically began with which process?
A. Prospective utilization review
B. Retrospective utilization review
C. Prospective utilization management
D. Retrospective utilization management

What are the six essential inquiries during discharge rounds?

B.
Healthcare utilization and resource allocation have evolved over time. This process began with retrospective, not prospective, utilization review. It then moved to utilization management, which is a prospective, proactive process that ensures, before the care is rendered, that effective and efficient care will be given.

1. What is the expected discharge date?
2. Can the client's current care and services be provided in another setting and/or at another level of care?
3. What needs are anticipated at discharge? What unanticipated needs may have to be addressed at discharge?
4. Based on the client's current status, what are the actual and potential barriers to discharge?
5. How can these actual and potential barriers be minimized and/or eliminated, and who will address them?
6. What are the next steps? When should the client be reevaluated?

Which of these four strategies is NOT part of utilization management?
  A. Utilization review
  B. Disease management
  C. Demand management
  D. Criteria review

The client's needed _____ depends on a number of factors including the severity of his/her disease or disorder, the presence of comorbidities, and other factors.

D.

Utilization management consists of four strategies: demand management, utilization review, case management, and disease management. Case managers review criteria, including reimbursement criteria, but this is not one of the four strategies associated with utilization management.

level of care

Reimbursement criteria are based on:
A. Length of stay
B. Laws and recommendations
C. Medical necessity
D. Medical quality

In the past, hospitals were reimbursed for care based on the services rendered. This form of reimbursement was referred to as _____ reimbursement.

C.

Reimbursement criteria are based on medical necessity. The role of the case manager is to continuously confirm that all clients are at the appropriate level of care and are being provided only those services consistent with these established criteria without compromising quality and positive patient outcomes.

retrospective

Initial authorizations for hospitalization usually:
A. Lead to rejections and appeals
B. Approve a one-time DRG payment
C. Include payment for comorbidities
D. Include payment for unanticipated needs

With _____ reimbursement, healthcare organizations are reimbursed based on a fixed rate attached to the client's DRG.

B.
Medicare, Medicaid, and other insurance companies usually grant initial certification that ensures a one-time payment based on the patient's diagnosis, which is also known as a diagnosis-related group (DRG) payment. Ongoing, concurrent authorizations are requested throughout the client's course of care and treatment to ensure adequate reimbursement for comorbidities and unanticipated client needs.

prospective

The best way to avoid denials is to:
   A. Employ a case manager
   B. Use appropriate resources
   C. Prevent them
   D. Appeal them

_____ provides healthcare reimbursement for adults ages 65 and older and permanently disabled people and their dependents.

C.

The best way to avoid denials and the need for appeals is to proactively prevent them with preventative measures. For example, when a length of stay at an acute care facility is not medically necessary, the client should be moved to another level of care. Denials are costly; appeals are also costly in terms of staff time. The best method is prevention, and the nursing case manager plays a very important role in this prevention.

Medicare

The primary reason that a healthcare organization should have an established policy and procedure for appeals is to ensure _____.
A. Accountability
B. Responsibility
C. Timely action
D. Case management evaluation

_____ provides healthcare reimbursement for low-income individuals and families and for chronically ill children.

C.

The primary reason that a healthcare organization should have an established policy and procedure for appeals is to ensure timely action. Usually, an appeal must be filed within 30-60 days of a denial notification. Insurance companies must then reply and respond to that appeal within 30-60 days after the appeal is filed. Although this may seem like a long time for the appeal process, all mechanisms must be in place and all parties involved ready to act without hesitation or the deadline can easily be missed.

Medicaid

Most facilities name one person, or position, to receive denials and possible denials of reimbursement. What does this ensure?
A. Accountability and responsibility
B. Successful appeals
C. Timely and complete appeals
D. Case manager participation in appeals

True or False: U.S. law mandates that worker's compensation and reimbursement for all treatments and care be given when a person sustains an injury or illness at work.

A.
Most facilities name one person, or position, to receive denials and possible denials of reimbursement because this establishes accountability and responsibility, and it prevents confusion and chaos. This key person will then notify the appropriate individuals, as also established in the facility's policy and procedure on denials and appeals.

True. The injured employee and his/her healthcare insurer do not pay for services covered by worker's compensation. Some examples of health conditions covered by worker's compensation are back injuries and infectious diseases.

You are the only nursing case manager in the facility. You notice that several denials have occurred among myocardial infarction clients. What should you do first?

A. Develop a quality improvement study to analyze the problem
B. Meet with all stakeholders to inform them of corrective measures
C. Call the third-party payer and negotiate the denials with them
D. Analyze the data and define the problem based on that data

Because Medicare, Medicaid, and private insurance companies need a justification for the rental or purchase of reusable medical equipment (such as walkers, wheelchairs, and prostheses), the client's independent practitioner (such as a medical doctor, physician's assistant, or nurse practitioner) must submit a _____.

D.

The first thing that you should do is analyze the data and define the problem based on that data. Denial data should be tracked and trended over time to prevent future denials. When trends are analyzed with aggregated data, the variables leading to the denials can be clearly identified and corrected to prevent future denials.

Certificate of Medical Necessity

Which level of care options along the continuum of care are listed from the least acute to the most acute?

A. Intensive care, cardiac step down, and home care
B. Cardiac step down, intensive care, and acute care
C. Home care, sub-acute care, and acute care
D. Assisted living, home care, and acute care

_____ involves assessing and evaluating the healthcare needs of a patient after an illness for which they were treated in a hospital or clinic.

C.

Home care, sub-acute care, and acute care are the level of care options that are listed in the proper sequence from the least acute to the most acute. In totality, levels of care from the most acute (and most costly) to the least acute (and least costly) are emergency departments and critical care areas, progressive or "step-down" acute care areas, acute care areas, sub-acute and rehabilitation centers, skilled nursing long-term care, assisted living, home care, and independent living.

Transitional planning

Which of the following is a criterion set that is used for utilization management?
A. InterQual criteria
B. IntraQual criteria
C. MediQual criteria
D. MetaQual criteria

What is the goal of transition planning?

A.
The InterQual® criteria sets for sub-acute care, inpatient rehabilitation, and skilled nursing facilities help case managers determine discharges and transfers to the safest, most clinically appropriate, most cost effective, and most efficient level of care based on critical thinking and professional judgment.

To transition a patient from one level of care to the next level as needed.

Which expression best exemplifies prospective reimbursement?
    A. "The more you do, the more you get."
    B. "Money in, money out."
    C. "Everything after admission is overhead."
    D. "The longer they stay, the more you get."

Who benefits from the case manager acting as a coordinator of care?

C.
"Everything after admission is overhead." As soon as the client is authorized for admission, the facility will receive a fixed payment based on the DRG. When more services are rendered and when the patient stays longer, profits and reimbursement are reduced.

The client, his/her family, the healthcare team, the organization, and the third-party payer

Which multidisciplinary plan of care is often used by case managers?
  A. Standardized care plan
  B. Critical pathway
  C. Individualized care plan
  D. Multidisciplinary pathway

The _____ involves many healthcare providers including clinical providers, services such as physical therapists and medical doctors, and supportive services and departments such as laboratory and other diagnostic services.

B.
The multidisciplinary plan of care that is often used by case managers is a critical, or clinical, pathway. These pathways, often referred to as multidisciplinary action plans, are a concrete way to plan and document client care that is consistent with the prospective reimbursement system's DRGs and reimbursable lengths of stay.

coordination of care

When a physical therapist has not provided planned services to a client because the client has refused them, it is documented in a critical pathway as what?

A. Variation
B. Variability
C. Variance
D. Verification

What are some impacting factors on the coordination of services?

C.

It is a variance when a physical therapist has not provided planned services to a client because the client refused them. A variance occurs when the client condition does not permit a planned intervention or activity, when a healthcare provider alters care to meet an individual's unanticipated need, when a test is not completed and reported in the established time frame, and/or when a clinical indicator or goal is not achieved. These four variances are referred to as patient-related, provider-related, organization-related, and clinical indicator-related, respectively.

The level of acuity, the nature of the illness or disorder, the client's psychosocial supports and support network, and the extent of the client's insurance coverage

Critical, or clinical, pathways are time-oriented. In intensive care units, what is the usual time frame?

A. Day-by-day
B. Hour-by-hour
C. Minute-by-minute
D. Shift-to-shift

True or False: Case management and critical pathways are based on the fact that most patients with a specific healthcare problem, illness, or health event are treated and respond to treatment in the same manner.

B.

Critical pathways in the critical care, or intensive care, unit are typically hourly because the patent's status is critical and often unstable. In non-critical care areas, the time frame is day-by-day (Day 1, Day 2, Day 3, etc.) rather than shift-by-shift.

True. For example, a patient who has undergone a total knee replacement is expected to experience some degree of pain and discomfort post-operatively for several days. He/she is also expected to have NO respiratory abnormalities related to immobility.

The beginnings of continuous quality improvement and performance improvement activities began decades ago with _____.

A. Outcomes measurements
B. Process measurements
C. Quality control
D. Quality assurance

_____, often referred to as multidisciplinary action plans, are a concrete way to plan and document client care that is consistent with the prospective reimbursement system's DRGs and reimbursable lengths of stay.

C.
The beginnings of continuous quality improvement and performance improvement activities began decades ago with quality control, which later evolved into quality assurance and most recently, into continuous quality improvement and performance improvement activities. These activities have also evolved from structure measurements to process measurements and finally, outcomes measurements.

Critical pathways

Which is an example of a core quality indicator (or measure)?
   A. JCAHO's ORYX
   B. Lengths of stay
   C. Morbidity rates
   D. Mortality rates

What are some elements that should be included in a critical pathway, or multidisciplinary action plan?

A.
Core measures are standardized measures of quality. The JCAHO has ORYX National Hospital Quality Measures that include disease-related measures for heart failure and pneumonia, population measures such as pediatric care, and organizational measures like those used in emergency departments.

- Consultations
- Diagnostic tests
- Client activity
- Treatments
- Medications
- Diet
- Discharge planning
- Nursing diagnoses and interventions
- Patient outcomes

Which is an example of an outcome measure?
   A. JCAHO's ORYX
   B. Medicaid outcomes indicator
   C. Medicare outcomes indicator
   D. Length of stay measurement

A _____ occurs when a client's condition does not permit a planned intervention or activity, when a healthcare provider alters care to meet an individual's unanticipated need, when a test is not done and reported in the established time frame, and/or a clinical indicator or goal is not achieved.

D.

Outcomes measures, unlike core measures, measure the outcomes of care. For example, lengths of stay, mortality and morbidity rates, and readmissions may be analyzed as outcome measures.

variance

Although risk management is closely aligned with continuous quality improvement, it differs from continuous quality improvement in which way?

A. Risk management proactively addresses opportunities for improvement.
B. Risk management reduces legal liability.
C. Risk management retroactively addresses opportunities for improvement.
D. Risk management is required by the JCAHO.

What do successful quality management and performance improvement activities accomplish?

B.
Although risk management is closely aligned with continuous quality improvement, it differs from continuous quality improvement in that risk management reduces legal liability related to events such as falls, elopement, infant abduction, and a wide variety of medical errors. Both processes are proactive and required by the JCAHO.

They improve the outcomes of care, improve the safety and efficiency of processes, reduce costs, and reduce risks and liability.

Root cause analysis can successfully determine which of the following?
   A. The individual who made a mistake
   B. The people who made a mistake
   C. Why nosocomial infections occur
   D. Problematic processes

_____ activities include identifying an opportunity to improve a process, organizing a team to improve an activity, identifying customer expectations and outcomes, gathering data and information, using best practices and research studies, analyzing the data, closely examining the existing process, designing the process with measurable specifications that can be evaluated, eliminating all variances, implementing the newly designed process, evaluating the improvement in terms of the measurable specifications, and documenting the entire procedure that led to the process change.

D.

Root cause analysis can successfully determine problematic processes. It determines the deepest, fundamental causes of mistakes and errors. These causes are procedures and processes, NOT people.

Continuous quality improvement

What is the term that describes an occurrence that leads to, or has the potential to lead to, an adverse outcome?

A. Adverse event
B. Cardinal event
C. Sentinel event
D. Variance

What are the two categories of quality indicators?

C.

Core measures and outcome measures

Which is a commonly occurring medical error?
A. Low levels of patient satisfaction
B. Suicide
C. Variance.
D. Practice that is inconsistent with standards

_____ measures are standardized measures of quality.

B.
The most commonly occurring medical errors are suicide, unintended retention of a foreign body after surgery or another invasive procedure, wrong patient/wrong site/wrong procedure, treatment delay, operative and post-operative complication, fall, criminal event, medication error, perinatal death, and other unanticipated events.

Core

The case manager is performing a quality assurance study and notices that a variance occurs because of details inherent to the process. Which kind of variance is this?

A. Independent
B. Dependent
C. Random
D. Specific

A failure to use and report data relating to core measures will result in what?

C.
Variances can be random and specific. A random variance is one that occurs because of details inherent to the process. These variances occur each time the established process is carried out. Specific variances occur because of one specific part of the process. Both random and specific variances must be corrected and eliminated.

The lowering of CMS reimbursement

Which is an example of hard savings?
A. Avoiding the use of excessive supplies
B. Avoiding the use of unnecessary durable medical equipment
C. Saving staff overtime salaries
D. Negotiating with insurance companies for reimbursement of extended lengths of stay

_____ measures are used to examine the outcomes of care.

D.

Some examples of hard savings include the case manager negotiating the number of times or length of time the client can receive a specific service; preventing the use of unnecessary supplies, equipment, and other limited resources; and negotiating the length of stay for a hospitalized patient. Soft savings, or cost avoidances, are more difficult to measure and predict.

Outcome

Which fact about outcomes is accurate?
- A. Case managers should measure outcomes before worrying about processes.
- B. Outcomes are stable and predictable when the structure and process are stable.
- C. Outcomes always vary, and they are unpredictable.
- D. Outcomes will be stable when the structure is stable, regardless of process.

_____ is closely aligned with continuous quality improvement, but instead of proactively planning change like quality improvement does, it aims to reduce liability by eliminating risks and liabilities that can include client-related risks, quality risks, and financial risks and liabilities.

B.
Outcomes are stable and predictable when the structure and process are stable. Erratic structures and/or erratic processes lead to erratic outcomes.

Risk management

In the case management component of _____, case managers identify and seek out clients who require case management services. One way that case managers find cases is with biopsychosocial screening to identify clients who are at risk or are in the early stages of a biopsychosocial needs process. In this component, the case manager assesses and interviews these clients to ensure that they are eligible and able to benefit from case manager services.

A. Case finding
B. Assessment and diagnosis
C. Service planning and resource identification
D. Linking clients to needed services

What are the main concepts behind risk management?

A.

Identifying potential risks; determining the likelihood of a risk, the effects of a risk, and the cost associated with a risk; and considering how the risk can be controlled and eliminated.

In the case management component of _____, the nursing case manager assesses the client and family to determine their biopsychosocial needs, strengths and weaknesses, and potential barriers to care.

A. Service planning and resource identification
B. Linking clients to needed services
C. Service implementation and care coordination
D. Assessment and diagnosis

In addition to client-related risks, institutions face _____ risks associated with faulty equipment, hazardous materials and waste, fire, and security issues.

D.

environmental

In the case management component of _____, the case manager collaborates with the client, family, and other members of the healthcare team to determine the care, services, and resources that are best for the client, within the limits of reimbursement. A critical pathway or multidisciplinary plan of action is the best way to document this plan.

A. Linking clients to needed services
B. Service planning and resource identification
C. Service implementation and care coordination
D. Monitoring care and variance analysis

_____ is a process used to determine the deepest, fundamental causes of mistakes and errors.

B.

Root cause analysis

In the case management component of _____, case managers link clients to the services that are needed. For acute care hospitalized patients, these resources are typically found within the facility. In long-term care facilities, however, these resources are often external to the facility. This requires that the client be transported for the delivery of services.

A. Service implementation and care coordination
B. Monitoring care and variance analysis
C. Linking clients to needed services
D. Evaluation

True or False: These causes found by root cause analysis are usually procedures and processes, not people.

C.

True

In the case management component of _____, the case manager coordinates, supervises, and concurrently evaluates the timeliness, effectiveness, and appropriateness of care.

A. Service implementation and care coordination
B. Monitoring care and variance analysis
C. Evaluation
D. Case finding

A _____ is an occurrence that leads to, or has the potential to lead to, an adverse outcome.

A.

sentinel event

In the case management component of _____, any deviations from the plan and expected outcomes are identified, analyzed, and corrected.

A. Evaluation
B. Monitoring care and variance analysis
C. Case finding
D. Assessment and diagnosis

True or False: When a client has a left leg amputation instead of a right leg amputation, the situation is a sentinel event has occurred.

B.

True

In the case management component of _____, case managers are accountable and responsible for evaluating the effectiveness of individual care and the overall effectiveness of the case management program and strategies.

A. Case finding
B. Assessment and diagnosis
C. Service planning and resource identification
D. Evaluation

True or False: When a nurse is about to administer an incorrect medication or dosage, then suddenly realizes the error and corrects it, a sentinel event has NOT occurred.

D.

False. Even "near-misses" are considered sentinel events.

The _____ manages the care of patients with the same diagnosis-related group throughout the organization without any restrictions such as the location of the client within the facility.

A. Collaborative Practice Model
B. Triad Model of Case Management
C. Case Manager Model (Beth Israel Multidisciplinary Patient Care Model)
D. Professionally Advanced Care Team (ProACT) Model

What are some of the most commonly occurring medical error sentinel events?

A.

Suicide, unintended retention of a foreign body after surgery or other invasive procedure, wrong patient/wrong site/wrong procedure, treatment delay, suicide, operative and post-operative complication, fall, criminal event, medication error, perinatal death, and other unanticipated events.

The _____ aims to decrease lengths of stay, increase patient and staff satisfaction, improve quality of care, and control the use of resources.

A. Disease Management Models
B. Triad Model of Case Management
C. Case Manager Model (Beth Israel Multidisciplinary Patient Care Model)
D. Collaborative Practice Model

_____ and the identifying best practices are superior ways that quality and risk can be objectively determined.

C.

Benchmarking

The _____, also referred to as the Collaborative Care Model, emphasizes close collaboration among a nursing case manager, social worker, and utilization review team member. The aim of this model is to move clients along the continuum of care by identifying and resolving system barriers and issues that thwart this movement.

A. Professionally Advanced Care Team (ProACT) Model
B. Triad Model of Case Management
C. Disease Management Models
D. Case Manager Model (Beth Israel Multidisciplinary Patient Care Model)

What are the four types of variances?

B.

Practitioner variance, system/institutional variance, community variance, and patient/family variance

In the _____, the nurse role is differentiated into two components: clinical case manager and primary nurse. The nurse's case management role consists of several functions including personnel, clinical, managerial, and fiscal accountability. Restructuring the nursing department included maximizing supportive, ancillary services with new and different roles to allow the nursing staff to exclusively provide those services that only nurses can provide.

A. Collaborative Practice Model
B. Triad Model of Case Management
C. Disease Management Models
D. Professionally Advanced Care Team (ProACT) Model

_____ variances occur because of inherent process details; these variances occur each time the established process is carried out.

D.

Random

_____ focus on specific diseases and evidence-based practices used to manage the costs and quality of the care provided to patients with specific diseases or disorders.

A. Disease Management Models
B. Collaborative Practice Model
C. Professionally Advanced Care Team (ProACT) Model
D. Triad Model of Case Management

_____ variances occur because of one specific part of the process.

A.

Specific

The _____ role dimension of case management includes reimbursement authorizations and certifications, preventing and addressing denials, cost control, utilization and resource management, cost containment, variance identification, analysis, and corrective actions.

A. Financial and business
B. Professional development
C. Management and leadership
D. Information management and communication

In the context of critical pathways, _____ is described as a deviation from the expected.

A.

managed care plan variance

The _____ role dimension of case management includes multidisciplinary and patient/family communication and collaboration, research, group leading, data entry and analysis, data management and retrieval, reports, and other methods of written communication.

A. Professional development
B. Information management and communication
C. Management and leadership
D. Financial and business

Why are variances documented?

B.

To enable future, or concurrent, data collection and analysis to improve processes.

The _____ role dimension of case management includes self-professional development activities and the development of the professional advancement of others within the organization and in the community.

A. Clinical and patient care
B. Management and leadership
C. Information management and communication
D. Professional development

_____ compares and contrasts the benefits and costs associated with an intervention.

Cost-benefit analysis

The _____ role dimension of case management includes patient identification and outreach, client assessment, problem identification, plan of care implementation, ongoing client reassessment, outcomes of care evaluation, and patient and family education.

A. Professional development
B. Financial and business
C. Clinical and patient care
D. Management and leadership

True or False: At times, insurance companies will request a cost-benefit analysis to justify reimbursement.

C.

True

The _____ role dimension of case management includes coordination of care; transitional and discharge planning; referrals; monitoring and supervision of care; patient advocacy; mentoring, coaching, and educating staff; active participation in and leadership of committees; development of continuous improvement activities relating to the case management program; and development and continuous improvement of critical, or clinical, pathways.

A. Financial and business
B. Management and leadership
C. Professional development
D. Information management and communication

Examples of _____ savings include the case manager negotiating the number of times or length of time the client can receive a specific service; preventing the use of unnecessary supplies, equipment, and other limited resources; and negotiating the length of stay for a hospitalized patient.

B.

hard

The American Case Management Association's Standards of Practice for a nursing case manager include guidelines to fulfill which of the following case management responsibilities?
A. Resource management
B. Communication
C. Advocacy
D. All of the above

Examples of _____ savings include avoidances of costs such as medical supplies and equipment, avoidance of readmission costs, avoidance of visits to an emergency department, increases in quality of life, and patient satisfaction with the delivery of high-quality care.

D.

soft

The _____ phase of the nursing process includes data collection relating to client and family member biopsychosocial, spiritual, and cultural needs and also to strengths, weaknesses, and potential barriers to care.

A. Diagnosis
B. Planning
C. Assessment
D. Implementation

What are the two types of data?

C.

Quantitative and qualitative

The _____ phase of the nursing process includes analyzing assessment data to determine health-related problems and concerns, health-related risks, strengths and weaknesses relating to the client and significant others, actual and potential barriers to care, and appropriate nursing diagnoses relating to actual and potential healthcare concerns.

A. Planning
B. Implementation
C. Assessment
D. Diagnosis

The prevalence or incidence of falls and nosocomial infections are examples of _____ data.

D.

quantitative

The _____ phase of the nursing process includes establishing priorities, developing expected outcomes of care or goals, and selecting appropriate interventions to achieve these goals.

A. Planning
B. Assessment
C. Evaluation
D. Implementation

Patient satisfaction and quality of life are often anecdotal narrative comments. This data is considered _____ data.

A.

qualitative

The _____ phase of the nursing process includes actual performance of interventions and assessment of responses to care.

A. Evaluation
B. Implementation
C. Assessment
D. Planning

True or False: Outcomes will be unpredictable and filled with variances if the process and structure are unstable.

B.

True

The _____ phase of the nursing process is most similar to the assessment phase and cycles right back into it. Data relating to current client status is collected and compared to established expected outcomes of care or client goals. The conclusion drawn from this comparison reflects whether or not client goals were met. It also poses the question, "Should the plan of care be continued, modified, or terminated?"

A. Evaluation
B. Implementation
C. Planning
D. Diagnosis

True or False: Unstable processes and structures will NOT lead to unstable outcomes.

A.

False. Because outcomes will be unpredictable and filled with variances if processes and structures are unstable, unstable processes and structures will, in fact, lead to unstable outcomes.

_____ abuse can be bruises, bone fractures, burns, etc.
- A. Physical
- B. Sexual
- C. Psychological
- D. Financial

Case managers can, and should, measure outcomes relating to what?

A.

Biological problems, psychological status, quality of life, functional abilities, the prevention of infections, goal attainment, safety, and the occurrence of adverse events

_____ abuse includes any sexual contact with a minor or a person, even a spouse, who has not consented to the sexual activity.

A. Financial
B. Psychological
C. Sexual
D. Physical

Patient care practices and organization performance can be measured and evaluated. What will this process involve?

C.

Measuring performance over time to determine if planned changes have increased performance, measuring to identify problems and opportunities for improvement, and taking actions to strategically improve performance

_____ abuse includes actions such as verbal bullying and threats of harm.

A. Physical
B. Psychological
C. Financial
D. Sexual

True or False: Nursing case managers must be currently licensed to practice nursing in their state of practice.

B.

True

176

_____ abuse can consist of withholding funds from another person.

A. Psychological
B. Sexual
C. Physical
D. Financial

_____ ensures that the individual has completed nursing school, successfully passed the licensure examination, and continually met the requirements for re-licensure every two years.

D.

Licensure

The *Principles* of the Code of Professional Conduct for Case Managers require case managers to do which of the following?
A. Uphold the rights and dignity of clients
B. Maintain a professional and objective patient relationship
C. Obey all regulations and laws
D. All of the above

_____ reflect a competency, in a specialty area, that is more advanced than the competency needed for licensure.

D.

Certifications

The *Rules of Conduct* of the Code of Professional Conduct for Case Managers state that case managers will NOT do which of the following?

A. Falsify documents or applications
B. Violate ethical codes or principles
C. Engage in unprofessional conduct
D. All of the above

True or False: Documentation errors can lead to serious patient-related consequences including death.

D.

True

The *Standards for Professional Conduct* of the Code of Professional Conduct for Case Managers include which of the following?

A. Professional responsibility of competency, boundaries, and limitations
B. Adherence to all laws
C. Full disclosure and reporting of conflicts of interest
D. All of the above

True or False: Nursing case managers do NOT need to follow the legislated scope of practice for their state of practice.

D.

False. Nursing case managers MUST follow the legislated scope of practice for their state of practice.

_____ is the ethical principle wherein each unique individual has the right to make choices without coercion or undue influence of others. Case managers do not
impose their own beliefs, values, or opinions on the client; they accept all client choices without judging. The patient has the right to choose and/or refuse any and all treatments and interventions.

   A. Accountability
   B. Veracity
   C. Fidelity
   D. Autonomy

True or False: Although there are some small differences among the 50 states in terms of their nurse scopes of practice, they are very similar for the registered nurse, the licensed practical (or vocational) nurse, and the advanced practicing nurse.

D.

True

_____ is the ethical principle that means "do not harm," as in the Hippocratic Oath. Harm can be intentional or unintentional, as is the case when a client has an adverse reaction to a medication.

A. Non-maleficence
B. Justice
C. Beneficence
D. Fidelity

Nurses violate _____ statutes when they function in roles and aspects of care beyond their scope of practice.

A.

scope of practice

_____ is the ethical principle that means "do good." Doing good is more than just not doing any harm. On occasion, it can lead to unanticipated harm.

A. Autonomy
B. Beneficence
C. Accountability
D. Veracity

True or False: Unlicensed nurses who have failed to either reapply for their license or have had it revoked as part of disciplinary action and continue to practice nursing are guilty of practicing nursing without a license.

B.

True

The ethical principle of _____ requires fairness to all.
  A. Fidelity
  B. Non-maleficence
  C. Justice
  D. Accountability

True or False: Medical records are legal documents.

C.

True

192

_____ is the ethical principle of being faithful to one's promises. By the very nature of the implicit nurse-client relationship, the nurse must be faithful and true to his/her professional promises and responsibilities by providing high quality, safe care in a competent, scientifically grounded manner.

A. Fidelity
B. Autonomy
C. Beneficence
D. Non-maleficence

What are the purposes of documentation?

A.

Communication among members of the healthcare team, fulfillment of the legal requirements of Medicare's Conditions of Participation and reimbursement, and fulfillment of the mandates of external regulatory bodies such as the JCAHO and the state departments of health

_____ is the ethical principle of truthfulness. Nurses, and case managers, do not withhold the whole truth from clients.

A. Accountability
B. Veracity
C. Fidelity
D. Autonomy

What does good documentation facilitate?

B.

Optimal and timely communication among team members; complete and appropriate care; timeliness of care; prevention of errors of omission, commission, and duplication; and minimization of treatment delays

_____ is the ethical principle wherein nurses are accountable for all aspects of nursing care. They must answer to themselves, clients, and society for their actions and must also accept personal and professional consequences of those actions.

A. Accountability
B. Beneficence
C. Justice
D. Veracity

What are some characteristics of good documentation?

A.

Legibility, accuracy, completeness, timeliness, and professionalism

According to the American Hospital Association, all patients have the right to which of the following?
A. Respect and dignity
B. Privacy
C. Freedom from abuse and neglect
D. All of the above

Most documentation errors are errors of _____. This is where a nurse fails to document something that should have been documented.

D.

omission

The _____ domain of learning consists of both knowledge and understanding. The six levels of this domain are knowledge, comprehension, application, analysis, synthesis, and evaluation. Some of the teaching/learning strategies for this domain include online/computer-based learning, peer group discussions, reading material, and a discussion or lecture.

A. Affective
B. Psychomotor
C. Cognitive
D. Adaptive

Other documentation errors are errors of _____. This is where a nurse may document faulty assessment data that was related to one of the nurse's other patients.

C.

commission

The _____ domain of learning consists of "hands-on skills" such as correctly taking a blood pressure measurement and using a blood glucose monitor. The seven levels of this domain are perception, set, guided response, mechanism, complex overt response, adaptation, and origination. Some of the teaching/learning strategies for this domain include demonstration, return demonstration, and a video with a step-by-step demonstration of this specific skill.

A. Psychomotor
B. Cognitive
C. Adaptive
D. Affective

The _____ protects patients' rights to the privacy and confidentiality of all medical information, including electronic information, unless the client has consented to it in writing.

A.

Health Insurance Portability and Accountability Act

The _____ domain of learning includes the development of attitudes, beliefs, values, and opinions. The five levels of this domain are receiving, responding, valuing, organization, and characterization by a value or a value complex. The teaching/learning strategies for this domain include role playing and values clarification exercises.

A. Adaptive
B. Affective
C. Psychomotor
D. Cognitive

_____ is defined as an act of omission or commission that does not meet established standards of care and results in patient injury. This act can be intentional or unintentional and consists of four components: the damages to the patient, the duty owed to the patient, the duty that was breached, and the direct or indirect injury and damages caused by the breach.

B.

Malpractice

In _____ change theory, the force of facilitators of change must be stronger than the barriers to change. The phases of change are unfreezing, experiencing the change, and refreezing to the new change.

    A. Lippitt, Watson, and Westley's Seven Phases of Change
    B. Lewin's Force Field Analysis
    C. Havelock's Six Phases of Planned Change
    D. Chaos Theory

_____ is also an act of omission or commission that does not meet established standards of care. It can be intentional or unintentional and differs from malpractice because it lacks one or more of the essential elements such as injury and damages.

B.

Negligence

In _____ theory, the six phases are developing relationships, diagnosing the existing problem, collecting available resources, choosing a solution, garnering acceptance, and stabilizing the change.

A. Roger's Innovation-Decision Process
B. Chaos Theory
C. Havelock's Six Phases of Planned Change
D. Lewin's Force Field Analysis

True or False: Nurses, nursing case managers, and others are NOT obligated to report suspected child abuse or neglect, patient abuse or neglect, domestic violence, and elder abuse or neglect.

C.

False. Nurses, nursing case managers, and others ARE, in fact, obligated to report all abuses.

In _____ theory, the seven phases of change include the client's awareness of the need for change, the development of a change agent/client relationship, the problem defined, the goals established, the plan for change implemented, the change accepted, and the change agent/client relationship changed.

A. Lippitt, Watson, and Westley's Seven Phases of Change
B. Havelock's Six Phases of Planned Change
C. Chaos Theory
D. Roger's Innovation-Decision Process

What are the categories of abuse and neglect?

A.

Physical, psychological, and financial

In _____ change theory, the case manager, as the change agent, provides the client with the knowledge and information about the benefits of change during the five stages of knowledge, persuasion, decision, implementation, and confirmation.

A. Chaos Theory
B. Roger's Innovation-Decision Process
C. Lewin's Force Field Analysis
D. Havelock's Six Phases of Planned Change

Examples of _____ are deprivation of adequate food; isolation and imprisonment in the home; and failure to provide another with sufficient funds to purchase items, such as shampoo, when there are available funds to buy them.

213

B.

neglect

The _____ of change addresses the constantly changing environment that impacts the client as an open system. Case managers must always expect the unexpected and never assume that predicted outcomes will occur automatically.

A. Roger's Innovation-Decision Process
B. Havelock's Six Phases of Planned Change
C. Lippitt, Watson, and Westley's Seven Phases of Change
D. Chaos Theory

_____, also referred to as a conservatorship, refers to the legal process with which another person makes decisions for a person who is incapable of making sound decisions on his/her own.

D.

Guardianship

Which of the following is a type of evaluation in the teaching/learning process?

A. Formative
B. Summative
C. Cumulative
D. Both A and B

What are some alternatives to guardianship?

D.

Durable powers of attorney, healthcare surrogacy, and case/care management

Which of the following is NOT a unique learner characteristic?
  A. Learning styles and preferences
  B. Ethnicity
  C. Literacy
  D. Motivation and readiness

True or False: Legally appointed guardians have legal decision-making power in terms of accepting or rejecting treatment and end-of-life decisions.

B.

True

_____ barriers to learning can be overcome with slow, brief, simple, and understandable explanations.

A. Sensory
B. Psychological
C. Cognitive
D. Cultural

What does the ANA's Code of Ethics emphasize?

C.

The dignity and worth of all people (without discrimination), nurses' commitment to patients, advocacy, accountability, preservation of safety and patient rights, competency, provision of quality care, collaboration, and integrity of the nursing profession

_____ barriers to learning can be accommodated with large print materials and braille for the visually impaired; louder discussions with clients affected by a hearing impairment; and the use of assistive devices such as magnifiers, eyeglasses, and hearing aids.

A. Psychological
B. Sensory
C. Cognitive
D. Cultural

According to the ANA's Standards of Professional Performance, what must nurses do?

B.

Advocate for patients; resolve ethical issues; and report all suspicions revolving around impaired, incompetent, and/or illegal practice

_____ barriers to learning can be minimized by establishing trust, reinforcing learning with positive feedback, and reducing stress.

A. Cognitive
B. Sensory
C. Cultural
D. Psychological

What are the ethical principles of case management?

D.

Autonomy and self-determination, non-maleficence, beneficence, justice, fidelity, veracity, and accountability

In the _____ model of health and wellness, the seven components of wellness are the physical, social, emotional, intellectual, spiritual, occupational, and environmental components of health.

A. Seven Components of Wellness
B. Role Performance Models
C. Adaptation Models
D. Health-Illness Continuum

_____ is the principle wherein patients must be fully informed and knowledgeable about the risks, benefits, and alternatives for all interventions and aspects of care.

A.

Informed consent

In _____ of health and wellness, health is based on the client's ability to perform his/her multiples roles in society. A person who is able to fulfill these roles, despite the presence of an illness or disorder, is considered healthy.

A. Seven Components of Wellness.
B. Role Performance Models
C. Adaptation Models
D. Health-Illness Continuum

_____ and _____ contain the client's wishes about which treatments and interventions he/she does and does not want carried out when unable to competently provide these consents and rejections.

B.

Advanced directives and living wills

In _____ of health and wellness, health is defined by how the client is able to successfully cope and adapt flexibly when faced with a health problem. Health is facilitated by the development of coping skills.

A. Seven Components of Wellness
B. Role Performance Models
C. Adaptation Models
D. Health-Illness Continuum

_____ in healthcare occurs when a nurse, or another healthcare provider, does not attend to the patient and his/her needs.

C.

Abandonment

In the _____ model of health and wellness, levels of health vary along the continuum, with high level wellness at one end of the continuum and death on the opposite end. Movement toward the wellness end of the continuum is facilitated by awareness, education, and growth.

A. Seven Components of Wellness
B. Role Performance Models
C. Adaptation Models
D. Health-Illness Continuum

_____ in healthcare occurs when a nurse, or another healthcare provider bills for services not rendered, receives or gives kickbacks, and/or bills for substandard care.

D.

Fraud

The _____ of health and wellness consists of two axes—horizontal health axis and vertical environment axis—and four quadrants—high-level wellness in a very favorable environment, emergent high-level wellness in an unfavorable environment, protected poor health in a favorable environment, and poor health in an unfavorable environment.

A. High-Level Wellness Model
B. Agent-Host-Environment Model
C. Health-Belief Model
D. Neumann's Systems Model

Although fraud and abuse can occur in all aspects and levels of care, thorough _____ can help to limit them.

A.

documentation

The _____ of health and wellness recognizes the presence of multiple variables, or causes, of disease. The *agent* is an internal or external environmental force that can lead to disease or illness. For example, bacterial pathogens cause infections. The *host* is the client or group that is susceptible to a particular illness because of one or more risk factors such as genetics. The *environment* consists of external factors that promote or impair health such as an exposure to toxic chemicals.

A. High-Level Wellness Model
B. Agent-Host-Environment Model
C. Health-Belief Model
D. Neumann's Systems Model

What are the three domains of learning that are the basis of all education (including patient and family education)?

B.

Cognitive, psychomotor, and affective

The _____ of health and wellness addresses the relationship of the client's perceptions, behaviors, and health. This model can predict whether or not a person will engage in screening tests, as based on his/her personal perceptions and beliefs. Perceived seriousness and threat can influence perceptions and health-related behaviors.

A. High-Level Wellness Model
B. Agent-Host-Environment Model
C. Health-Belief Model
D. Neumann's Systems Model

_____ is childhood learning.

C.

Pedagogy

In _____ of health and wellness, the client, as an open system within the environment, tries to prevent any disruption, or penetration, of the system despite the presence of stressors. The client has a normal line of defense, lines of resistance, and flexible lines of defense.

A. High-Level Wellness Model
B. Agent-Host-Environment Model
C. Health-Belief Model
D. Neumann's Systems Model

_____ is adult learning.

D.

Andragogy

In the _____ of health and wellness, the six dimensions of health are biophysical (genetic composition, physical risk factors, and disease), psychological (coping mechanisms), behavioral (lifestyle choices such as nutrition), physical environment (air pollutants), socio-cultural (societal norms and beliefs), and health systems (accessibility, availability, and affordability).

A. Neumann's Systems Model
B. Holistic Models
C. Pender's Health Promotion Model
D. Dimension Model

What are the differences between pedagogy and andragogy?

D.

Unlike pedagogy, andragogy has immediate usefulness in terms of solving problems; it involves active learner involvement and participation, and the curriculum and content are based on the learner's needs and desires.

In _____ of health and wellness, the client's level of motivation and commitment is impacted by the client's characteristics, emotions, and behavior-specific cognitions.

A. Neumann's Systems Model
B. Holistic Models
C. Pender's Health Promotion Model
D. Dimension Model

What are the three types of change?

C.

Technical, structural, and people-oriented

In _____ of health and wellness, holistic approaches to health and wellness facilitate the case manager's consideration of all aspects of the client's status (physical, psychological, social, and spiritual) and all interrelationships of those aspects. This care focuses on educating the person so that he/she can take responsibility for achieving balance and well-being in his/her life. It promotes a belief in the ability of clients to control or, at least, participate in the planning of their lives if given the necessary knowledge, skills, and support.

A. Neumann's Systems Model
B. Holistic Models
C. Pender's Health Promotion Model
D. Dimension Model

_____ evaluation is the continuous assessment of the effectiveness of the teaching while the teaching is being conducted.

B.

Formative

_____ prevention focuses on the prevention of health problems, disease, and dysfunction before they occur. Some of the components of this type of prevention are health promotion activities such as identifying risks and specific protections. Examples include eliminating safety risks and immunizing against infectious diseases.

A. Primary
B. Secondary
C. Tertiary
D. Quaternary

_____ evaluation occurs at the end of the learning activity and allows the case manager to determine whether or not the education has achieved the established learning objectives for the individual or group.

A.

Summative

_____ prevention involves the early identification, or diagnosis, and treatment of specific health problems, complications, and disabilities. Examples include screening procedures for breast cancer and colon cancer.

A. Primary
B. Secondary
C. Tertiary
D. Quaternary

What are some of the common issues associated with patient education?

B.

Information about health insurance benefits, treatment options and alternatives, the benefits and risks associated with different interventions, and available resources including community resources.

_____ prevention aims to return the client to the highest possible level of functioning after the treatment, or correction, of a health problem. Examples include rehabilitation and restorative care activities, such as retraining, and exercise to limit functional disability.

A. Primary
B. Secondary
C. Tertiary
D. Quaternary

What are the three levels of illness prevention?

C.

Primary, secondary, and tertiary

CPSIA information can be obtained
at www.ICGtesting.com
Printed in the USA
LVOW01s1128040816
499065LV00024B/174/P